CONTENTS

COPYRIGHT……….2
DISCLAIMER……….3
INTRODUCTION……….4
NCLEX ® STUDY GUIDE QUESTIONS……….6
ANSWERS & RATIONALE……….17
QUESTIONS & ANSWERS……….24
NCLEX ® ESSENTIALS……….43

NCLEX ® REVIEW

Copyright © 2016

Paperback Edition

All rights reserved. No part of this publication may be reproduced, distributed, stored in a retrieval system or transmitted in any form or by any means, including photocopying, recording, or other electronic or mechanical methods, without the prior written permission of the publisher.

The right of High Cedar Press to be identified as the authors of the work has been asserted in accordance with the Copyright, Designs and Patents Act 1988.

Illustrations Copyright © 2016

DISCLAIMER

The full contents of 'NCLEX ® REVIEW', including text, comments, graphics, images, and other content are for informational purposes only and does not imply legal, medical, financial or other advice. The information is not intended to diagnose, treat, cure or prevent any illnesses or diseases. Always consult you physician for all matters concerning your health.

This study guide is for practice purposes only. It is not a representation of the NCLEX ® exam. Doing well on these practice questions does not guarantee success on your real exam. Use this guide to highlight areas that need further revision.

This study guide is intended to give further practice for the NCLEX ® text, but keep in mind not all material or topics you are responsible for is covered within this guide. Medicine and nursing is constantly changing, as are the topics featured within the exam each year so it is the reader's responsibility to check the syllabus.

The author has tried to make the questions and answers as accurate as possible, however cannot be responsible for any errors or inaccuracies. It is the reader's responsibility to check all information.

Every effort has been made to prepare this material to ensure it's accuracy, however the author nor publisher will not be held responsible if there is information deemed as inaccurate.

NCLEX ® are registered trademarks of National Council of State Boards of Nursing, INC and hold no affiliation with this product.

INTRODUCTION

If you are here reading this book you are more than likely preparing to conquer the 'dreaded' NCLEX ® Exam. Well let me tell you that you are not alone and have nothing to worry about! With the correct study methods, focus and time you will be sure to ace the test! This study guide is here to help relieve your stress by allowing you to practice questions which may occur in the real exam. Another purpose of this book is to highlight which areas you may need to brush up on.

My suggestion is to take this test as if you were taking the real thing. Mark yourself to obtain a score - then have a look at the areas you may need to brush up on. Once you have gone over the areas you have not have done as well on, you can give the practice questions another go to hopefully boost your confidence and assure you that the exam isn't the 'beast' you may think it is!

The study guide is split up into 4 sections:

SECTION 1: QUESTIONS. You should use this section as you would a real test. Sit down in peace and quiet- take out a piece of paper and write your answers down.

SECTION 2: ANSWERS. Marking your practice exam will be quick and easy. Remember to give yourself a score then look back over the answers you got incorrect. It is recommended you write down the areas you were unable to answer correctly. Go over these areas so that when you come back to this book to repeat the practice exam you will be sure to ace it!

SECTION 3: QUESTIONS & ANSWERS. You may prefer to look back at the test with the answer on the page so you can reread them all as you go along.

SECTION 4: STUDY GUIDE ESSENTIALS. This section features a guide of potential subjects and areas which may come up on the test. It is small 'bite-sized' pieces of information presented in a simple way to make revising much easier for you. It is worth going through all of these very carefully and re-writing them on either flashcards or within a notepad so that you can look back over them.

Please note that this book is simply a guide - it is in no way an indication of what you may have on your exam, nor is it a definitive guide featuring all topics. Various other topics and questions may arise on the test that are not featured within this book....however this book it is a great starting point!

Here's to wishing you the best of luck! And if you are feeling nervous always remember 'Doubt kills more dreams than failure ever will."

NCLEX ® STUDY GUIDE QUESTIONS

1. What is the recommended daily caloric intake for a moderately active man?

    A. 2200 calories
    B. 2800 calories
    C. 1600 calories
    D. 1800 calories

2. What is the recommended daily caloric intake for adult women?

    A. 2100 calories
    B. 2300 calories
    C. 1800 calories
    D. 2000 calories

3. What is the recommended daily caloric intake for an active teenage boy?

    A. 2800 calories
    B. 2600 calories
    C. 3000 calories

D. 2000 calories

4. Of the women below, who is at greatest risk of having a child with a cleft lip and palate?

   A. A 19-year-old Indian woman who is having a boy.
   B. A 46-year-old Caribbean woman who is having a girl.
   C. A 28-year-old Native American woman who is having a boy.
   D. A 30-year-old Scandinavian woman who is having a girl.

5. Place Abraham Maslow's Hierarchy of Human Needs in order, with 1 being the most important and 5 being the least important.

   A. Safety and Psychological Needs
   B. Love and Belonging
   C. Self-Actualization
   D. Physiological Needs
   E. Self Esteem

6. RACE is an acronym used to help staff when responding to a fire emergency. Put the following steps in the correct order.

   A. Confine the fire by closing any door or windows
   B. Attempt to safely extinguish the fire using a fire extinguisher
   C. Pull the nearest fire alarm

D. Remove anyone in danger

7. A patient admitted to the psychiatric unit is claiming to be an angel sent from God with a mass of followers. Which of the following is the most likely cause:

   A. He is experiencing a stressful period in his life
   B. Inflated self-esteem
   C. Low self-esteem
   D. He has just returned from a religious event

8. Which of the following improves the quality of iron absorption?

   A. Protein
   B. Calcium
   C. Potassium
   D. Vitamin C

9. You are treating a schizophrenic patient with echolalia. Which of the following would be a common behaviour?

   A. Speaking with a significantly louder tone of voice
   B. Inability to form coherent sentences
   C. Speak at a rapid pace
   D. Repetition of the noises or phrases used by others

10. During your shift, you suspect that another licensed nurse is verbally and physically abusing a patient. What should you do?

    A. Carry on working and deal with this incident after your shift
    B. Call the authorities
    C. Immediately report the incident to the charge nurse
    D. Nothing, as you only suspect the abuse and have no proof

11. Which of the following are signs or symptoms of hyperthyroidism?

    A. Weight Loss
    B. Increased sweating
    C. Constipation
    D. Thinning hair

12. Which of the following is used to assess a patient's' risk for skin breakdown?

    A. The Glasgow Scale
    B. The Morse Scale
    C. The Norton Scale
    D. The Snellen Scale

13. Which liquid should you place an avulsed tooth in?

A. Boiling water
B. Milk
C. Room temperature water
D. Saline

14. During pregnancy, the embryonic period begins during:

    A. Weeks 6 to 10
    B. Weeks 5 to 10
    C. Weeks 2 to 8
    D. Weeks 3 to 5

15. During pregnancy, the ovulation period begins during:

    A. Weeks 2 to 3
    B. Weeks 5 to 6
    C. Weeks 1 to 2
    D. Weeks 4 to 5

16. During pregnancy, the first trimester runs from:

    A. Week 1 to 4
    B. Week 4 to 8
    C. Week 1 to 12
    D. Week 12 to 14

17. During which week does the fetus begin to develop hands, eyes and legs?

A. Week 2
B. Week 5
C. Week 9
D. Week 3

18. How frequently do feeding times commonly occur for a newborn?

A. Every 3 hours
B. Every 4 hours
C. Every 2 hours
D. Every 1 hour

19. Which of the following is the most nutrient dense element of breast milk produced during the postpartum stage?

A. Colostrum
B. Progesterone
C. Prolactin
D. Estrogen.

20. At what age will surgical correction for an infant who has a cleft palate take place?

A. 4 to 8 months
B. 2 to 4 months
C. 20 to 24 months

D. 8 to 12 months

21. What is the normal adult sodium level?

   A. 4 to 9 milliequivalents
   B. 135 to 145 milliequivalents
   C. 135 to 145 micro equivalents.
   D. 4 to 9 micro equivalents.

22. Select from the following the potential complications which may arise from immobility:

   A. Shallow respirations
   B. Urinary stasis
   C. Stiff and painful joints
   D. A negative calcium balance
   E. All of the above

23. Which of the following is considered an adventitious breath sound?

   A. Fine rales
   B. Vesicular breath sounds
   C. Tracheal
   D. Bronchovesicular

24. What is deemed to be the most important factor to consider when communicating with children?

A. Behavioral cues
B. Development level
C. Physical development
D. Parental relationship and involvement

25. A patient is recommended to increase their daily intake of potassium. Which of the following is the best source of potassium?

A. Banana
B. Orange
C. Apple
D. Grapes

26. When consumed, which of the following provides the highest risk of gastric cancer?

A. Cheese
B. Sugar
C. Processed meats
D. Vegetable Oil

27. According to the Denver Developmental Screening Test which of the following behaviours is an example of the normal gross motor skills of a 2-year-old?

A. The child can draw a vertical line
B. The child can jump

C. The child can form a coherent sentence
   D. The child can place a toy in front or behind her

28. With regards to the gross motor skills of the toddler, which of the following is the most suited activity?

   A. Kicking a ball
   B. Playing with building blocks
   C. Going down a slide
   D. Using a skipping rope

29. Which of the below are used to treat patients that have been treated with heavy metal poisonings, such as iron or lead?

   A. Bismuth subsalicylate
   B. Activated charcoal
   C. Antiemetics
   D. Chelating agents

30. Which of the below could be used to prevent vomiting?

   A. Antiemetics
   B. Ipecac syrup
   C. Chelating agents
   D. IV infusions of oxytocin

31. Which of the below is commonly associated with end-stage renal failure?

A. Weight loss
B. Pruritis
C. Increased energy
D. Hair loss

32. It is recommended that a patient suffering from Meniere's syndrome follows a diet plan that is:

A. High in calcium
B. High in fiber
C. Low in iodine
D. Low in sodium

33. If a patient has a gluten-induced enteropathy, which of the following snacks would be most suitable?

A. Pitta bread
B. Oatmeal
C. Popcorn
D. Pretzels

34. Which of the following is best to alleviate itching and irritations associated with varicella?

A. Rubbing the affected area with an antiseptic
B. Applying a paste-like mixture of baking soda and water
C. Gently applying a clean cloth soaked in milk
D. Running the irritated area under cold water

35. At which time and at which dose is recommendation for administering Zantac (ranitidine)?

    A. One dose before breakfast and one before bed
    B. One dose on an empty stomach
    C. One dose at bedtime or with meals
    D. Three doses, one after each meal

36. Which of the following foods should be avoided if a patient has been diagnosed with oxalate renal calculi?

    A. Rhubarb
    B. Spinach
    C. Strawberries
    D. Apples

37. Of the below, which would you associate with an increased risk of colorectal cancer?

    A. High in fat and refined carbohydrates
    B. Low in protein and high in complex carbohydrates
    C. High in refined carbohydrates and low protein
    D. High in complex carbohydrates and low in complex proteins

38. When treating a patient with an iron-deficiency which of the following foods would not provide an adequate source of iron?

   A. Chickpeas
   B. Tomatoes
   C. Poultry
   D. Spinach

39. When treating a patient who frequently feels cold after being diagnosed with hypothyroidism, the best recommendation would be:

   A. Dresses in extra layers of clothing
   B. Sleep next to a radiator or heater
   C. Take a hot bath at least once per day
   D. Go for a walk outdoors, even in the winter

40. What is most likely to have caused the development of laryngeal cancer?

   A. A long-term infection that was never diagnosed
   B. A poor diet
   C. Frequent use of alcohol and tobacco
   D. Genetics

41. You have a patient who has been diagnosed with rheumatoid arthritis. Which of the following activities would you recommend in order to ease symptoms?

   A. Taking pain medicine frequently
   B. Smoking to relieve stress
   C. Taking a warm bath
   D. Consuming alcohol to ease the pain

42. What is the average weight of a newborn baby?

   A. 10 pounds
   B. 8 pounds
   C. 7 pounds
   D. 11 pounds

43. Digoxin (Lanoxin) is commonly used to treat congestive heart failure. Which of the below is NOT a desired symptom from the treatment?

   A. Slows down or regulates the heart rate
   B. Increased urinary output
   C. Loss of appetite
   D. Improves blood circulation

44. A patient has been diagnosed with iron deficiency anemia. Which of the following is the best advice to give this patient when they are discharged?

A. Take the medicine when you wake up on an empty stomach
B. Take the medicine with antacids
C. Take the medicine along with some form of dairy. e.g. cheese or milk
D. Take the medicine at breakfast with a whole grain cereal

45. Which of the following statements would lead you to suspect a toddler has iron-deficient anemia?

A. The toddler drinks a lot of milk, around 2- 3 cups per day
B. The toddler refuses to eat raw vegetables
C. The toddler drinks a lot of juice each day. The amount is likely to exceed 8 ounce
D. per day
A. The toddler dislikes meat and refuses to eat it even in small quantities

46. What is a symptom commonly associated with acute adrenal crisis?

A. High sodium
B. Low blood pressure
C. Constipation
D. Facial flushing

47. Which of the following symptoms is an indication of pneumonia?

   A. Increased heart rate
   B. Sneezing
   C. Fever and chills
   D. Skin sensitivity

48. What does the term "blue bloater" refer to?

   A. Chronic obstructive bronchitis
   B. Iron-deficient anemia
   C. Asthma
   D. Pneumonia

49. What would be a common symptom of a patient with chronic obstructive bronchitis?

   A. They would appear bloated in their chest
   B. They would have a rash on their skin
   C. They would have chronic headaches
   D. They would suffer from frequent nosebleeds

50. Which diet is most suited to a patient following an episode of pancreatitis?

   A. Low in calories and high in complex carbohydrates
   B. Low in protein and high in fat

C. High in protein and low in fat
   D. High in calories and low in fat

51. Which of the following actions, if performed by a nurse, would be considered negligence?

   A. The nurse takes a blood sample from a 4-day-old newborn without the parent present.
   B. The nurse instructs an elderly patient diagnosed with asthma to blow on a whistle.
   C. The nurse massages lotion on the stomach of a toddler diagnosed with Wilms tumour.
   D. The nurse asks a patient diagnosed with juvenile arthritis to run a short distance outdoors.

52. An alcoholic patient enters the emergency room and is suffering from acute alcohol withdrawal. Which is the following should be administered?

   A. Methadone hydrochloride (Dolophine)
   B. Codeine Phosphate (Co-codamol)
   C. Naproxen (Naprosyn)
   D. Chlordiazepoxide hydrochloride (Librium)

53. A patient with hypertension attended a class a month ago in order to help him quit smoking. During their follow-up consultation, the nurse notices a packet of cigarette in his pocket. Which would be the most appropriate response?

A. "The class was only a month ago, did you not learn anything?"
B. "I noticed a packet of cigarettes in your pocket."
C. "You can expect a call from your physician to discuss this further"
D. "Quitting smoking is hard, well done for trying anyway."

54. Which of the following is a long-term complication of diabetes mellitus?

    A. Hypoglycemia
    B. Diabetic ketoacidosis
    C. Hyperosmolar Hyperglycaemic State
    D. Retinopathy

55. Which of the following behaviours are indicative of panic level of anxiety?

    A. Distorted perception, behavioral disorganization, heart palpitations.
    B. Behavioral disorganization, Reduced sensory input, reduced heart rate.
    C. Increased pulse, feeling cold, distorted perception.
    D. Heightened sensory awareness, inability to form coherent sentences, increased muscle tension.

56. A nurse is visiting an 84-year-old lady who lives with her son. The nurse suspects that the elderly lady may be malnourished and notices bruising on her legs. What would be the most appropriate response?

   A. Report the situation to a supervisor.
   B. Arrange a meeting the patient's family to discuss the situation.
   C. Organise for a home care nurse to visit the patient every day to observe the situation.
   D. Assume the elderly patient is clumsy with a lack of appetite and continues your days work.

57. A nurse is caring for a patient with symptoms of inappropriate antidiuretic hormone (SIADH). Which of the following would the patient experience?

   A. Decreased blood sodium, Decreased urine output, and hyponatremia with increased or normal plasma volume.
   B. Increased urine output, increased blood sodium, and hyponatremia with decreased plasma volume.
   C. Stable urine output, decreased blood sodium and hyponatremia with increased plasma volume.
   D. Stable blood sodium, decreased urine output, and hyponatremia with normal or decreased plasma volume.

58. Which of the following tests would indicate a patient's hydration levels?

   A. Red blood cell count (RBC).
   B. Hematocrit (Hct).
   C. Hypertension diagnosis.
   D. Urine specific gravity.

59. Of the patients below, who has the lowest risk of developing deep vein thrombosis (DVT)?

   A. An overweight 40-year-old woman weighing 240 lbs living a sedentary lifestyle.
   B. A 60-year-old builder undergoing knee replacement surgery.
   C. A 50-year-old woman who has undergone surgery to remove her cataracts.
   D. A 70-year-old woman with breast cancer undergoing treatment from chemotherapy.

60. Upon discharging a patient after cataract surgery which of the following should be advised?
   A. The eye shield should be worn during the day if pain or irritation occurs.
   B. Prescribed eye drops should be used.
   C. Take one dose of the prescribed pain relief medication twice a day.
   D. The patient must wear dark glasses at all times.

ANSWERS & RATIONALE

1. ANSWER: B. 2800
An active older man would require around 400 calories less, and a sedentary younger man would require around 2400.

2. ANSWER: D. 2000
The calorie intake for an inactive adult woman is around 1800, and for an older woman (over 50) is around 1600.

3. ANSWER: A. 2800
A sedentary teenage boy would require 400 calories less. An active teenage girl requires 2400, and an inactive teenage girl is recommended to consume approx. 1600-1800 calories per day.

4. ANSWER: C
A 28-year-old Native American woman who is having a boy. The highest prevalence rates for a cleft lip and palate have been reported for Native Americans.

5. ANSWER:
D. Physiological needs
A. Safety and psychological needs

Love and Belonging
E. Self Esteem
C. Self-Actualization

6. ANSWER:
D. RESCUE
C. ALARM
A. CONTAIN
B. EXTINGUISH / EVACUATE (only if it is small. If you are unable to safely extinguish the fire, evacuate the area immediately)

7. ANSWER: C. Low self-esteem
A false impression of one's own importance is commonly associated with low self-esteem.

8. ANSWER: D. Vitamin C
Food rich in vitamin C such as spinach, kale and other dark green vegetables along with citrus fruit, tomatoes and strawberries improve the absorption of iron - providing they are eaten at the same time as iron-rich foods.

9. ANSWER: D. Repetition of the noises or phrases used by others
Other symptoms of schizophrenia include delusions, disorganised speech or behaviour and hallucinations.

10. C. Immediately report the incident to the charge nurse

All cases of suspected abuse involving patients are required by law to be reported.

11. A. Weight Loss, B. Increased Sweating, D. Thinning Hair
Other symptoms may include diarrhea, difficulty sleeping, skin thinning, nervousness and an increased heart rate.

12. C. The Norton Scale
The Glasgow Scale assesses the conscious state of an individual. The Morse Scale is a fall risk assessment. The Snellen Scale is an eye chart used to measure visual acuity.

13. B. Milk
Milk is commonly used as a preservation fluid when an avulsed tooth cannot be reimplanted immediately. Milk is relatively free of bacterial contamination and is isotonic.

14. A. Weeks 6 to 10
The embryonic period is approximately 8 weeks from fertilisation and will continue to week 10. This is the earliest stage of development.

15. C. Weeks 1 to 2
The ovulation period commonly begins around and 14 days before a menstrual cycle.

16. C. Week 1 until week 12

The second trimester begins around week 13 to week 28 and the third trimester is usually around week 29 to week 40.

17. B. Week 5

18. C. Every 2 hours. On average newborns require feeding every 1-2 hours, between 8-12 per day.

19. A. Colostrum
Progesterone is a hormone that plays an important role in maintaining the early stages of pregnancy. Prolactin aides the production of breast milk. Estrogen is the primary female hormone and is present in all females, not only pregnant women.

20. D. 8-12 months
Surgery for a cleft lip will occur at 4-6 months and for a cleft palate surgery will take place between 8-12 months. This is to reduce the duration of feeding problems caused by the surgery.

21. B. 135 to 145
A normal sodium level for an adult is f 135 to 145 mEq/L(milliequivalents per liter).

22. E. All of the above.
Other complications which may arise from immobility include a reduction in circulation, increased pressure on legs, low blood pressure and a greater risk of edema.

23. A. Fine Rales
'Fine rales' or crackles heard from a patient's lungs. Other adventitious breathing sounds include wheezes (rhonchi), pleural rubs, stridor and stertor.

24. B. Development level
This is the most important element to consider when determining how to communicate with the child.

25. A. Banana
Other sources of potassium include sweet and white potatoes, tomatoes (cooked), yoghurt and tuna.

26. C. Processed Meats
The link between processed meats including lunch meat, salami, bacon and hot dogs and cancer prove that individuals are at a higher risk when consuming these types of food.

27. D. The child can place a toy in front or behind her.
Gross motor skills are related to a child's ability to move and coordinate their arms and legs. Fine motor skills are associated with smaller movements within the wrists, fingers and toes.

28. A. Kicking a ball
Kicking a ball is the most suited activity from the list above to assess a child's gross motor skills as it relates to larger

movements the child's makes with their legs, arms or the entire body.

29. D. Chelating agents
Bismuth subsalicylate or Pepto-Bismol is used to treat issues related to the stomach such as heartburn or nausea. Activated charcoal is charcoal that has been heated in order to increase its absorption so would not help treat metal poisoning. Antiemetic is an antinauseant used to treat vomiting.

30. A. Antiemetics
Ipecac syrup is used to induce vomiting. Chelating agents form bonds with metals and can be used to treat metal poisoning. Oxytocin is a hormone.

31. B. Pruritis
End-stage renal failure is the last stage of kidney disease. Pruritis is severe skin irritation and itching. Other symptoms may include swollen ankles, nausea and shortness of breath.

32. D. Low in sodium.
Meniere's syndrome can cause vertigo and tinnitus. Consuming too much sodium increases fluid within the body, making the symptoms worse.

33. C. Popcorn

All types of corn is gluten free. The other options within the list of answers contain moderate to high levels or gluten and should be avoided.

34. B. Baking soda mixed with water. This is a popular home remedy that can cause itching to subside.

35. C. One dose at bedtime or with meals

36. A, B & C - Rhubarb, Strawberries and Spinach
A low - oxalate diet is recommended for patients diagnosed with oxalate renal calculi.   Oxalate is naturally found in many foods including rhubarb, spinach, strawberries, peanuts, beetroot and sweet potatoes.

37. A. High in fat and refined carbohydrates

38. B. Tomatoes.
Tomatoes are a low source of iron with only 0.3mg per 100g.

39. A. Dress in extra layers of warm clothing
Sleeping next to a radiator can cause burns if it is set too high and the skin comes into contact with it during the night. A patient suffering from hypothermia must be gradually warmed - it is very dangerous to put them in a hot bath. Avoid going out in cold weather as this will low the body temperature further.

40. C. Frequent use of alcohol and tobacco

The use of tobacco and alcohol is linked to cancer of the throat.

41. C. Taking a warm bath.
Pain medicine is not necessary for a patient with arthritis. Smoking or alcohol consumption is never encouraged as it will cause other health problems. Taking a warm bath will help to ease joints and alleviate discomfort.

42. C. 7 pounds

43. C. Loss of appetite
Slowing or regulating the heart rate, increased urinary output and improved blood circulation are all desired symptoms.

44. A. Take the medicine when you wake up on an empty stomach
A patient could also take the medication along with vitamin C. Antacids, whole grains and calcium may interfere with the absorption of iron.

45. A and C
If the child is drinking such large quantities of milk or juice is likely that the parent is neglecting to provide their toddler with other essential nutrients.

46. B. Low blood pressure
Other symptoms may include severe vomiting and diarrhea, loss of consciousness and dehydration.

47. C. Fever and Chills
Other symptoms may include snaking, shortness of breath, coughing and chest pains.

48. A. Chronic obstructive bronchitis
Patients diagnosed with chronic obstructive pulmonary disease have been split into two groups: 'Pink Puffers' and 'Blue Bloaters'. This is based on their physiological response to the symptoms of the disease. A 'Pink Puffer' refers to a patient with emphysema.

49. A. They would appear bloated in their chest
Chronic obstructive bronchitis is caused by damage to the lungs over many years which causes the airways to get inflamed, leading to bloatedness and excess production of mucus.

50. D. High in calories and low in fat

51. C. The nurse massages lotion on the stomach of a toddler diagnosed with Wilms Tumour.
Rubbing the tumour may cause cancer to spread.

52. D. Chlordiazepoxide hydrochloride (Librium).
Librium is used to calm the nervous system and is administered to patients suffering from alcohol withdrawal.

53. B. "I noticed a packet of cigarettes in your pocket."
This response allows the nurse to engage in a further discussion with the patient.

54. D. Retinopathy
Retinopathy related to eye damage and could potentially lead to blindness. It is common for a diabetes sufferer to have damaged blood vessels of the retina (diabetic retinopathy).

55. A. Distorted perception, behavioral disorganization, heart palpitations.
Other symptoms of a panic-level anxiety attack may include shaking, shortness of breath, feeling dizzy or faint or chest pains.

56. A. Report the situation to a supervisor
A supervisor will be able to take the matter further and by law, this matter must be reported.

57. A. Decreased urine output, decreased serum sodium, and hyponatremia with normal or increased plasma volume.

58. B & D. Hematocrit and Urine specific gravity.

59. C. A 50-year-old woman who has undergone surgery to remove her cataracts.
All other answers would leave the patient's relatively immobile and at greater risk of developing DVT.

60. B. Prescription eye drops should be used.
It is not necessary to use an eye mask when in pain, however using a mask at night may prevent any accidents. Pain relief is not needed as cataract surgery is painless.

QUESTIONS & ANSWERS

1. What is the recommended daily caloric intake for a moderately active man?

    A. 2200 calories
    B. 2800 calories
    C. 1600 calories
    D. 1800 calories

ANSWER: B. 2800
An active older man would require around 400 calories less, and a sedentary younger man would require around 2400.

2. What is the recommended daily caloric intake for adult women?

    A. 2100 calories
    B. 2300 calories
    C. 1800 calories
    D. 2000 calories

ANSWER: D. 2000
The calorie intake for an inactive adult woman is around 1800, and for an older woman (over 50) is around 1600.

3. What is the recommended daily caloric intake for an active teenage boy?

   A. 2800 calories
   B. 2600 calories
   C. 3000 calories
   D. 2000 calories

ANSWER: A. 2800
A sedentary teenage boy would require 400 calories less. An active teenage girl requires 2400, and an inactive teenage girl is recommended to consume approx. 1600-1800 calories per day.

4. Of the women below, who is at greatest risk of having a child with a cleft lip and palate?

   A. A 19-year-old Indian woman who is having a boy.
   B. A 46-year-old Caribbean woman who is having a girl.
   C. A 28-year-old Native American woman who is having a boy.
   D. A 30-year-old Scandinavian woman who is having a girl.

ANSWER: C
A 28-year-old Native American woman who is having a boy. The highest prevalence rates for a cleft lip and palate have been reported for Native Americans.

5. Place Abraham Maslow's Hierarchy of Human Needs in order, with 1 being the most important and 5 being the least important.

    A. Safety and Psychological Needs
    B. Love and Belonging
    C. Self-Actualization
    D. Physiological Needs
    E. Self Esteem

ANSWER:
D. Physiological needs
A. Safety and psychological needs
Love and Belonging
E. Self Esteem
C. Self-Actualization

6. RACE is an acronym used to help staff when responding to a fire emergency. Put the following steps in the correct order.

    A. Confine the fire by closing any door or windows
    B. Attempt to safely extinguish the fire using a fire extinguisher
    C. Pull the nearest fire alarm
    D. Remove anyone in danger

Answer:

D. RESCUE
C. ALARM
A. CONTAIN
B. EXTINGUISH / EVACUATE (only if it is small. If you are unable to safely extinguish the fire, evacuate the area immediately)

7. A patient admitted to the psychiatric unit is claiming to be an angel sent from God with a mass of followers. Which of the following is the most likely cause:

   A. He is experiencing a stressful period in his life
   B. Inflated self-esteem
   C. Low self-esteem
   D. He has just returned from a religious event

ANSWER: C. Low self-esteem
A false impression of one's own importance is commonly associated with low self-esteem.

8. Which of the following improves the quality of iron absorption?

   A. Protein
   B. Calcium
   C. Potassium
   D. Vitamin C

ANSWER: D. Vitamin C
Food rich in vitamin C such as spinach, kale and other dark green vegetables along with citrus fruit, tomatoes and strawberries improve the absorption of iron - providing they are eaten at the same time as iron-rich foods.

9. You are treating a schizophrenic patient with echolalia. Which of the following would be a common behaviour?

    E. Speaking with a significantly louder tone of voice
    F. Inability to form coherent sentences
    G. Speak at a rapid pace
    H. Repetition of the noises or phrases used by others

ANSWER: D. Repetition of the noises or phrases used by others
Other symptoms of schizophrenia include delusions, disorganised speech or behaviour and hallucinations.

10. During your shift, you suspect that another licensed nurse is verbally and physically abusing a patient. What should you do?

    A. Carry on working and deal with this incident after your shift
    B. Call the authorities
    C. Immediately report the incident to the charge nurse

D. Nothing, as you only suspect the abuse and have no proof

ANSWER: C. Immediately report the incident to the charge nurse
All cases of suspected abuse involving patients are required by law to be reported.

11. Which of the following are signs or symptoms of hyperthyroidism?

   A. Weight Loss
   B. Increased sweating
   C. Constipation
   D. Thinning hair

ANSWER: A. Weight Loss, B. Increased Sweating, D. Thinning Hair
Other symptoms may include diarrhea, difficulty sleeping, skin thinning, nervousness and an increased heart rate.

12. Which of the following is used to assess a patient's' risk for skin breakdown?

   A. The Glasgow Scale
   B. The Morse Scale
   C. The Norton Scale
   D. The Snellen Scale

ANSWER: C. The Norton Scale

The Glasgow Scale assesses the conscious state of an individual. The Morse Scale is a fall risk assessment. The Snellen Scale is an eye chart used to measure visual acuity.

13. Which liquid should you place an avulsed tooth in?

    A. Boiling water
    B. Milk
    C. Room temperature water
    D. Saline

ANSWER: B. Milk

Milk is commonly used as a preservation fluid when an avulsed tooth cannot be reimplanted immediately. Milk is relatively free of bacterial contamination and is isotonic.

14. During pregnancy, the embryonic period begins during:

    A. Weeks 6 to 10
    B. Weeks 5 to 10.
    C. Weeks 2 to 8.
    D. Weeks 3 to 5.

ANSWER: A. Weeks 6 to 10

The embryonic period is approximately 8 weeks from fertilisation and will continue to week 10. This is the earliest stage of development.

15. During pregnancy, the ovulation period begins during:

    A. Weeks 2 to 3
    B. Weeks 5 to 6
    C. Weeks 1 to 2
    D. Weeks 4 to 5

ANSWER: C. Weeks 1 to 2
The ovulation period commonly begins around and 14 days before a menstrual cycle.

16. During pregnancy, the first trimester runs from:

    A. Week 1 to 4
    B. Week 4 to 8
    C. Week 1 to 12
    D. Week 12 to 14

ANSWER: C. Week 1 until week 12
The second trimester begins around week 13 to week 28 and the third trimester is usually around week 29 to week 40.

17. During which week does the fetus begin to develop hands, eyes and legs?

A. Week 2
B. Week 5
C. Week 9
D. Week 3

Answer: B. Week 5

18. How frequently do feeding times commonly occur for a newborn?

A. Every 3 hours
B. Every 4 hours
C. Every 2 hours
D. Every 1 hour

ANSWER: C. Every 2 hours. On average newborns require feeding every 1-2 hours, between 8-12 per day.

19. Which of the following is the most nutrient dense element of breast milk produced during the postpartum stage?

A. Colostrum
B. Progesterone
C. Prolactin
D. Estrogen.

ANSWER: A. Colostrum

Progesterone is a hormone that plays an important role in maintaining the early stages of pregnancy. Prolactin aides the production of breast milk. Estrogen is the primary female hormone and is present in all females, not only pregnant women.

20. At what age will surgical correction for an infant who has a cleft palate take place?

    A. 4 to 8 months
    B. 2 to 4 months
    C. 20 to 24 months
    D. 8 to 12 months

ANSWER: D. 8-12 months
Surgery for a cleft lip will occur at 4-6 months and for a cleft palate surgery will take place between 8-12 months. This is to reduce the duration of feeding problems caused by the surgery.

21. What is the normal adult sodium level?

    A. 4 to 9 milliequivalents
    B. 135 to 145 milliequivalents
    C. 135 to 145 micro equivalents.
    D. 4 to 9 micro equivalents.

Answer: B.

A normal sodium level for an adult is f 135 to 145 mEq/L(milliequivalents per liter).

22. Select from the following the potential complications which may arise from immobility:

   A. Shallow respirations
   B. Urinary stasis
   C. Stiff and painful joints
   D. A negative calcium balance
   E. All of the above

ANSWER: E. All of the above.
Other complications which may arise from immobility include a reduction in circulation, increased pressure on legs, low blood pressure and a greater risk of edema.

23. Which of the following is considered an adventitious breath sound?

   A. Fine rales
   B. Vesicular breath sounds
   C. Tracheal
   D. Bronchovesicular

ANSWER: A. Fine Rales

Fine rales or crackles heard from a patient's lungs. Other adventitious breathing sounds include wheezes (rhonchi), pleural rubs, stridor and stertor.

24. What is deemed to be the most important factor to consider when communicating with children?

    A. Behavioral cues
    B. Development level
    C. Physical development
    D. Parental relationship and involvement

ANSWER: B. Development level
This is the most important element to consider when determining how to communicate with the child.

25. A patient is recommended to increase their daily intake of potassium. Which of the following is the best source of potassium?

    A. Banana
    B. Orange
    C. Apple
    D. Grapes

ANSWER: A. Banana
Other sources of potassium include sweet and white potatoes, tomatoes (cooked), yoghurt and tuna.

26. When consumed, which of the following provides the highest risk of gastric cancer?

　　A. Cheese
　　B. Sugar
　　C. Processed meats
　　D. Vegetable Oil

ANSWER: C. Processed Meats
The link between processed meats including lunch meat, salami, bacon and hot dogs and cancer prove that individuals are at a higher risk when consuming these types of food.

27. According to the Denver Developmental Screening Test which of the following behaviours is an example of the normal gross motor skills of a 2-year-old?

　　A. The child can draw a vertical line
　　B. The child can jump
　　C. The child can form a coherent sentence
　　D. The child can place a toy in front or behind her

ANSWER: D. The child can place a toy in front or behind her. Gross motor skills are related to a child's ability to move and coordinate their arms and legs. Fine motor skills are associated with smaller movements within the wrists, fingers and toes.

28. With regards to the gross motor skills of the toddler, which of the following is the most suited activity?

   A. Kicking a ball
   B. Playing with building blocks
   C. Going down a slide
   D. Using a skipping rope

ANSWER. A. Kicking a ball
Kicking a ball is the most suited activity from the list above to assess a child's gross motor skills as it relates to larger movements the child's makes with their legs, arms or the entire body.

29. Which of the below are used to treat patients that have been treated with heavy metal poisonings, such as iron or lead?

   A. Bismuth subsalicylate
   B. Activated charcoal
   C. Antiemetics
   D. Chelating agents

ANSWER: D. Chelating agents
Bismuth subsalicylate or Pepto-Bismol is used to treat issues related to the stomach such as heartburn or nausea. Activated charcoal is charcoal that has been heated in order to increase its absorption so would not help treat metal poisoning. Antiemetic is an antinauseant used to treat vomiting.

30. Which of the below could be used to prevent vomiting?

   A. Antiemetics
   B. Ipecac syrup
   C. Chelating agents
   D. IV infusions of oxytocin

ANSWER: A. Antiemetics
Ipecac syrup is used to induce vomiting. Chelating agents form bonds with metals and can be used to treat metal poisoning. Oxytocin is a hormone.

31. Which of the below is commonly associated with end-stage renal failure?

   A. Weight loss
   B. Pruritis
   C. Increased energy
   D. Hair loss

ANSWER: B. Pruritis
End-stage renal failure is the last stage of kidney disease. Pruritis is severe skin irritation and itching. Other symptoms may include swollen ankles, nausea and shortness of breath.

32. It is recommended that a patient suffering from Meniere's syndrome follows a diet plan that is:

A. High in calcium
B. High in fiber
C. Low in iodine
D. Low in sodium

ANSWER: D. Low in sodium.
Meniere's syndrome can cause vertigo and tinnitus. Consuming too much sodium increases fluid within the body, making the symptoms worse.

33. If a patient has a gluten-induced enteropathy, which of the following snacks would be most suitable?

A. Pitta bread
B. Oatmeal
C. Popcorn
D. Pretzels

ANSWER: C. Popcorn
All types of corn is gluten free. The other options within the list of answers contain moderate to high levels or gluten and should be avoided.

34. Which of the following is best to alleviate itching and irritations associated with varicella?

A. Rubbing the affected area with an antiseptic
B. Applying a paste-like mixture of baking soda and water

C. Gently applying a clean cloth soaked in milk
D. Running the irritated area under cold water

ANSWER: B. Baking soda mixed with water. This is a popular home remedy that can cause itching to subside.

35. At which time and at which dose is recommendation for administering Zantac (ranitidine)?

    A. One dose before breakfast and one before bed
    B. One dose on an empty stomach
    C. One dose at bedtime or with meals
    D. Three doses, one after each meal

ANSWER: C. One dose at bedtime or with meals

36. Which of the following foods should be avoided if a patient has been diagnosed with oxalate renal calculi?

    A. Rhubarb
    B. Spinach
    C. Strawberries
    D. Apples

ANSWER: A, B & C - Rhubarb, Strawberries and Spinach
A low - oxalate diet is recommended for patients diagnosed with oxalate renal calculi. Oxalate is naturally found in many

foods including rhubarb, spinach, strawberries, peanuts, beetroot and sweet potatoes.

37. Of the below, which would you associate with an increased risk of colorectal cancer?

   A. High in fat and refined carbohydrates
   B. Low in protein and high in complex carbohydrates
   C. High in refined carbohydrates and low protein
   D. High in complex carbohydrates and low in complex proteins

ANSWER: A. High in fat and refined carbohydrates

38. When treating a patient with an iron-deficiency which of the following foods would not provide an adequate source of iron?

   A. Chickpeas
   B. Tomatoes
   C. Poultry
   D. Spinach

ANSWER: B. Tomatoes.
Tomatoes are a low source of iron with only 0.3mg per 100g.

39. When treating a patient who frequently feels cold after being diagnosed with hypothyroidism, the best recommendation would be:

   A. Dresses in extra layers of clothing
   B. Sleep next to a radiator or heater
   C. Take a hot bath at least once per day
   D. Go for a walk outdoors, even in the winter

ANSWER: A. Dress in extra layers of warm clothing
Sleeping next to a radiator can cause burns if it is set too high and the skin comes into contact with it during the night. A patient suffering from hypothermia must be gradually warmed - it is very dangerous to put them in a hot bath. Avoid going out in cold weather as this will low the body temperature further.

40. What is most likely to have caused the development of laryngeal cancer?

   A. A long-term infection that was never diagnosed
   B. A poor diet
   C. Frequent use of alcohol and tobacco
   D. Genetics

ANSWER: C. Frequent use of alcohol and tobacco
The use of tobacco and alcohol is linked to cancer of the throat.

41. You have a patient who has been diagnosed with rheumatoid arthritis. Which of the following activities would you recommend in order to ease symptoms?

   A. Taking pain medicine frequently
   B. Smoking to relieve stress
   C. Taking a warm bath
   D. Consuming alcohol to ease the pain

ANSWER: C. Taking a warm bath.
Pain medicine is not necessary for a patient with arthritis. Smoking or alcohol consumption is never encouraged as it will cause other health problems. Taking a warm bath will help to ease joints and alleviate discomfort.

42. What is the average weight of a newborn baby?

   A. 10 pounds
   B. 8 pounds
   C. 7 pounds
   D. 11 pounds

ANSWER: C. 7 pounds

43. Digoxin (Lanoxin) is commonly used to treat congestive heart failure. Which of the below is NOT a desired symptom from the treatment?

A. Slows down or regulates the heart rate
B. Increased urinary output
C. Loss of appetite
D. Improves blood circulation

ANSWER: C. Loss of appetite
Slowing or regulating the heart rate, increased urinary output and improved blood circulation are all desired symptoms.

44. A patient has been diagnosed with iron deficiency anemia. Which of the following is the best advice to give this patient when they are discharged?

A. Take the medicine when you wake up on an empty stomach
B. Take the medicine with antacids
C. Take the medicine along with some form of dairy. e.g. cheese or milk
D. Take the medicine at breakfast with a whole grain cereal

ANSWER: A. Take the medicine when you wake up on an empty stomach
A patient could also take the medication along with vitamin C. Antacids, whole grains and calcium may interfere with the absorption of iron.

45. Which of the following statements would lead you to suspect a toddler has iron-deficient anemia?

　　B. The toddler drinks a lot of milk, around 2- 3 cups per day
　　C. The toddler refuses to eat raw vegetables
　　D. The toddler drinks a lot of juice each day. The amount is likely to exceed 8 ounces per day
　　E. The toddler dislikes meat and refuses to eat it even in small quantities

ANSWER: A and C
If the child is drinking such large quantities of milk or juice is likely that the parent is neglecting to provide their toddler with other essential nutrients.

46. What is a symptom commonly associated with acute adrenal crisis?

　　A. High sodium
　　B. Low blood pressure
　　C. Constipation
　　D. Facial flushing

ANSWER: B. Low blood pressure
Other symptoms may include severe vomiting and diarrhea, loss of consciousness and dehydration.

47. Which of the following symptoms is an indication of pneumonia?

    A. Increased heart rate
    B. Sneezing
    C. Fever and chills
    D. Skin sensitivity

ANSWER: C. Fever and Chills
Other symptoms may include snaking, shortness of breath, coughing and chest pains.

48. What does the term "blue bloater" refer to?

    A. Chronic obstructive bronchitis
    B. Iron-deficient anemia
    C. Asthma
    D. Pneumonia

ANSWER: A. Chronic obstructive bronchitis
Patients diagnosed with chronic obstructive pulmonary disease have been split into two groups: 'Pink Puffers' and 'Blue Bloaters'. This is based on their physiological response to the symptoms of the disease. A 'Pink Puffer' refers to a patient with emphysema.

49. What would be a common symptom of a patient with chronic obstructive bronchitis?

A. They would appear bloated in their chest
B. They would have a rash on their skin
C. They would have chronic headaches
D. They would suffer from frequent nosebleeds

ANSWER: A. They would appear bloated in their chest
Chronic obstructive bronchitis is caused by damage to the lungs over many years which causes the airways to get inflamed, leading to bloatedness and excess production of mucus.

50. Which diet is most suited to a patient following an episode of pancreatitis?

A. Low in calories and high in complex carbohydrates
B. Low in protein and high in fat
C. High in protein and low in fat
D. High in calories and low in fat

ANSWER: D. High in calories and low in fat

51. Which of the following actions, if performed by a nurse, would be considered negligence?

A. The nurse takes a blood sample from a 4-day-old newborn without the parent present.

B. The nurse instructs an elderly patient diagnosed with asthma to blow on a whistle.
C. The nurse massages lotion on the stomach of a toddler diagnosed with Wilms tumour.
D. The nurse asks a patient diagnosed with juvenile arthritis to run a short distance outdoors.

ANSWER: C. The nurse massages lotion on the stomach of a toddler diagnosed with Wilms Tumour.
Rubbing the tumour may cause cancer to spread.

52. An alcoholic patient enters the emergency room and is suffering from acute alcohol withdrawal. Which is the following should be administered?

A. Methadone hydrochloride (Dolophine)
B. Codeine Phosphate (Co-codamol)
C. Naproxen (Naprosyn)
D. Chlordiazepoxide hydrochloride (Librium)

ANSWER: D. Chlordiazepoxide hydrochloride (Librium). Librium is used to calm the nervous system and is administered to patients suffering from alcohol withdrawal.

53. A patient with hypertension attended a class a month ago in order to help him quit smoking. During their follow-up consultation, the nurse notices a packet of cigarette in his pocket. Which would be the most appropriate response?

A. "The class was only a month ago, did you not learn anything?"
B. "I noticed a packet of cigarettes in your pocket."
C. "You can expect a call from your physician to discuss this further"
D. "Quitting smoking is hard, well done for trying anyway."

ANSWER: B. I noticed a packet of cigarettes in your pocket. This response allows the nurse to engage in a further discussion with the patient.

54. Which of the following is a long-term complication of diabetes mellitus?

A. Hypoglycemia
B. Diabetic ketoacidosis
C. Hyperosmolar Hyperglycaemic State
D. Retinopathy

ANSWER: D. Retinopathy
Retinopathy related to eye damage and could potentially lead to blindness. It is common for a diabetes sufferer to have damaged blood vessels of the retina (diabetic retinopathy).

55. Which of the following behaviours are indicative of panic level of anxiety?

A. Distorted perception, behavioral disorganization, heart palpitations.
B. Behavioral disorganization, Reduced sensory input, reduced heart rate.
C. Increased pulse, feeling cold, distorted perception.
D. Heightened sensory awareness, inability to form coherent sentences, increased muscle tension.

ANSWER: A. Distorted perception, behavioral disorganization, heart palpitations.
Other symptoms of a panic-level anxiety attack may include shaking, shortness of breath, feeling dizzy or faint or chest pains.

56. A nurse is visiting an 84-year-old lady who lives with her son. The nurse suspects that the elderly lady may be malnourished and notices bruising on her legs. What would be the most appropriate response?

A. Report the situation to a supervisor.
B. Arrange a meeting the patient's family to discuss the situation.
C. Organise for a home care nurse to visit the patient every day to observe the situation.
D. Assume the elderly patient is clumsy with a lack of appetite and continues your days work.

ANSWER: A. Report the situation to a supervisor

A supervisor will be able to take the matter further and by law, this matter must be reported.

57. A nurse is caring for a patient with symptoms of inappropriate antidiuretic hormone (SIADH). Which of the following would the patient experience?

    A. Decreased urine output, decreased serum sodium, and hyponatremia with normal or increased plasma volume.
    B. Increased urine output, increased serum sodium, and hyponatremia with decreased plasma volume.
    C. Stable urine output, decreased serum sodium and hyponatremia with increased plasma volume.
    D. Stable serum sodium, decreased urine output, and hyponatremia with normal or decreased plasma volume.

ANSWER: A. Decreased urine output, decreased serum sodium, and hyponatremia with normal or increased plasma volume.

58. Which of the following tests would indicate a patient's hydration levels?

    A. Red blood cell count (RBC).
    B. Hematocrit (Hct).
    C. Hypertension diagnosis.
    D. Urine specific gravity.

ANSWER: B & D. Hematocrit and Urine specific gravity.

59. Of the patients below, who has the lowest risk of developing deep vein thrombosis (DVT)?

    A. An overweight 40-year-old woman weighing 240 lbs living a sedentary lifestyle.
    B. A 60-year-old builder undergoing knee replacement surgery.
    C. A 50-year-old woman who has undergone surgery to remove her cataracts.
    D. A 70-year-old woman with breast cancer undergoing treatment from chemotherapy.

ANSWER: C. A 50-year-old woman who has undergone surgery to remove her cataracts.
All other answers would leave the patient's relatively immobile and at greater risk of developing DVT.

60. Upon discharging a patient after cataract surgery which of the following should be advised?
    E. The eye shield should be worn during the day if pain or irritation occurs.
    F. Prescribed eye drops should be used.
    G. Take one dose of the prescribed pain relief medication twice a day.
    H. The patient must wear dark glasses at all times.

ANSWER: B. Prescription eye drops should be used.
It is not necessary to use an eye mask when in pain, however using a mask at night may prevent any accidents. Pain relief is not needed as cataract surgery is painless.

NCLEX ® ESSENTIALS

PRECAUTIONS & ROOM ASSIGNMENT

STANDARD PRECAUTIONS:

- Wash your hands
- Wear Gloves
- Gowns in case of any splashes
- Masks and Eye Protection
- Never recap needles
- Mouthpiece / Ambu-bag for resuscitation
- Refrain from giving care if you have skin abrasions / scratches etc

ALCOHOL WITHDRAWAL: Benzos (Lorazepam, Ativan etc)
- Tachypnea, Delirium Tremens (12-36 hrs after last drink), Tachycardia, Shakes, Paranoia, Nausea, Anxiety, Hallucinations

OPIATE WITHDRAWAL: Dilated pupils, Cramps, Hot & Cold Sweats, Watery Eyes, Low Energy, Runny Nose.

STIMULANTS WITHDRAWAL: Disrupted Sleep Patterns, Emotional Agility, Anxiety, Depression, Fatigue.

NUTRITION:

VITAMIN K: Milk, Meat, Soy, Dark Leafy Greens
VITAMIN C: Kiwis, Citrus Fruit, Bell Peppers, Tomatoes
VITAMIN A: Liver, Carrots, Sweet Potatoes, Tropical Fruits, Dark Leafy Greens
VITAMIN D: Egg Yolk, Beef Liver, Fatty Fish and Fish Oils, Sunshine
VITAMIN E: Almonds, Avocados, Dark Leafy Greens, Fish
FOLIC ACID: Dried Pulses, Lentils, Broccoli, Spinach, Okra
CALCIUM: Dairy Products, Dark Leafy Greens, Sardines

VITAMIN DEFICIENCY:

Pale Skin, Weight Loss, Shortness of Breath, Muscle Weakness, Nausea, Dizziness. Tingling in Hands or Feet.

BMI:
18.5 to 24.9 = Normal
Over 24.9 = Obese
Under 18.5 = Underweight

POST-OP:

- Sit up straight
- Breath in deeply through the nose and breath out slowly through pursed lips
- Hold breath for 3 seconds
- Cough 3 times (with the exception of patients with an abdominal wounds)

- Listen out for for Stridor (or other abnormal breathing sounds)
- Keep Tracheostomy kit close by
- Staples and sutures to be removed in 7-14 days (Keep dry until removed)
- Advise patient they cannot lift over 10 lbs for 6 weeks
- If a chest tube becomes disconnected place the free end into container of sterile water immediately
- When removing chest tube use the Valsalva maneuver, or ask the patient to draw in a deep breath and hold for a few seconds.
- If the patient gags while inserting a nasogastric tube allow them to calm down then try again while the patient sips water from a straw.

STAGES OF LABOUR:

STAGE 1 / EARLY LABOUR: Mild to moderate contractions every 30-45 seconds. Dilated Cervix
STAGE 2 / PUSHING STAGE: Cervix is fully dilated (10cm)
STAGE 3: Delivery of Placenta / Empty bags of water attached (membrane)
STAGE 4 / RECOVERY: 1 to 4 hours after delivery

MASLOW'S HIERARCHY OF NEEDS:

- Physiologic
- Safety
- Love and Belonging
- Self Esteem
- Self-actualization

ABC's:

- Airway
- Breathing
- Circulation

Thank you and best of luck with your exams!

www.ingramcontent.com/pod-product-compliance
Lightning Source LLC
LaVergne TN
LVHW011152260125
802194LV00035B/1477